*Private Diary of Joseph Smith
1832-1834*

By Joseph Smith

Copyright © 2021 Lamp of Trismegistus. All rights reserved. No part of this publication may be reproduced or transmitted in any form or by any means, electronic or mechanical, including photocopying, recording, or by any information storage and retrieval system, without permission in writing from Lamp of Trismegistus. Reviewers may quote brief passages.

ISBN: 978-1-63118-546-5

*Mormon History
Series*

Other Books in this Series and Related Titles

Pearl of Great Price by Joseph Smith (978-1-63118-539-7)

The Angel of the Prairies or A Dream of the Future: Mormon History Series
By Elder Parley Parker Pratt (978-1-63118-541-0)

A Manuscript on Far West by Reed Peck (978-1-63118-544-1)

The Story of Mormonism by James E Talmage (978-1-63118-543-4)

Interesting Account of Several Remarkable Visions: Mormon History Series
By Orson Pratt (978-1-63118-553-3)

An Address to All Believers in Christ Elder David Whitmer (978-1-63118-545-8)

The Philosophy of Mormonism by James E Talmage (978-1-63118-542-7)

The Book of Abraham: Mormon History by George Reynolds (978-1-63118-540-3)

The Testament of Abraham by Abraham (978-1-63118-441-3)

The Book of the Watchers by Enoch (978-1-63118-416-1)

The Evening and Morning Star Volume 1, Numbers 1 & 2 (978-1-63118-547-2)

The Evening and Morning Star Volume 1, Numbers 3 & 4 (978-1-63118-548-9)

The Evening and Morning Star Volume 1, Numbers 5 & 6 (978-1-63118-549-6)

The Evening and Morning Star Volume 1, Numbers 7 & 8 (978-1-63118-550-2)

The Evening and Morning Star Volume 1, Numbers 9 & 10 (978-1-63118-551-9)

The Evening and Morning Star Volume 1, Numbers 11 & 12 (978-1-63118-552-6)

The Testament of Moses by Moses (978-1-63118-440-6)

The Book of Parables by Enoch (978-1-63118-429-1)

The Secrets of Enoch by Enoch (978-1-63118-449-9)

The Book of Astronomical Secrets by Enoch (978-1-63118-443-7)

Audio Versions are also available on Audible, Amazon and Apple

Other Books in this Series and Related Titles

The Hidden Mysteries of Christianity by Annie Besant (978–1–63118–534–2)

American Indian Freemasonry by A C Parker (978-1-63118-460-4)

Rosicrucian Rules, Secret Signs, Codes and Symbols by various (978-1-63118-488-8)

History and Teachings of the Rosicrucians by W W Westcott &c (978-1-63118-487-1)

Freemasonry and the Egyptian Mysteries by C. W. Leadbeater (978-1-63118-456-7)

The Sepher Yetzirah and the Qabalah by M P Hall (978-1-63118-481-9)

The Psalms of Solomon by King Solomon (978-1-63118-439-0)

The Historic, Mythic and Mystic Christ by Annie Besant (978–1–63118–533–5)

Masonic and Rosicrucian History by M P Hall & H Voorhis (978-1-63118-486-4)

Some Deeper Aspects of Masonic Symbolism by A E Waite (978-1-63118-461-1)

Masonic Symbolism of King Solomon's Temple by A Mackey &c (978-1-63118-442-0)

The Old Past Master by Carl H Claudy (978-1-63118-464-2)

Book of Dreams by Enoch (978-1-63118-437-6)

The Mysteries of Freemasonry & the Druids by various (978-1-63118-444-4)

Masonic Symbolism of the Apron & the Altar by various (978-1-63118-428-4)

The Book of Wisdom of Solomon by King Solomon (978-1-63118-502-1)

Masonic Symbolism of Easter and the Christ in Masonry (978-1-63118-434-5)

The Odes of Solomon by King Solomon (978-1-63118-503-8)

Ancient Mysteries and Secret Societies by M P Hall (978-1-63118-410-9)

The Golden Verses of Pythagoras: Five Translations (978-1-63118-479-6)

A Few Masonic Sermons by A. C. Ward &c (978-1-63118-435-2)

Audio versions are also available on Audible, Amazon and Apple

Table of Contents

Diary of Joseph Smith, Jr. (1832-1834)

1832…7

1833…9

1834…19

1832

Joseph Smith Jrs Book for Record Baught on the 27th of November 1832 for the purpose to keep a minute acount of all things that come under my obse[r]vation &c

Oh may God grant that I may be directed in all my thaughts Oh bless thy Servent Amen

28 November 1832—Wednesday

this day I have [spent] in reading and writing this Evening my mind is calm and serene for which I thank the Lord God

29 November 1832—Thursday

this day road from Kirtland to Chardon to see my Sister Sop[h]ronia and also ca[lled] to see my Sister Catherine [and fou]nd them [well] this Evening Brother Frederic [G. Williams] Prophecyed that next spring I should go to the city of PittsBurg to establish a Bishopwrick and within one year I should go to the City of New York the Lord spare the life of thy servent Amen

30 November 1832—Friday

this day retu[r]ned home to Kirtland found all well to the Joy and satisfaction of my soul on my return home stopped at Mr Kings bore testmony to him and Family &c

1 December 1832—Saturday

bore testimony to Mr Gilmore wrote and corrected revelations &c

2 December 1832—Sunday

the sabath went to meeting &c

3 December 1832—Monday

ordaind Brother Packherd [Noah Packard] with my own hand also Brother umfiry [Solomon Humphrey] came to see me from the East & braught news from Brother Lyman Johnson and Orson Pratt &c. also held a conference in the Evening Br Jese [Jesse Gause?] and Mogan [Morgan?] and William Mclelen was excommunicated from the church &c

4 December 1832—Tuesday

this day I been unwell done but litle been at home all day regulated some things this Evening feel better in my mind then I have for a few days back Oh Lord deliver thy servent out of temtations and fill his heart with wisdom and understanding

5 December 1832—Wednesday

this day copying letters and translating and in evening held a council to advise with Brother Solomon Humphry it was ordered by the council that he should be a companion with Brother Noah packard in the work of the ministry

6 December 1832—Thursday

translating and received a revelation explaining the Parable [of] the wheat and the tears &c

1833

4 October 1833—Friday

makeing preperation to go East with Freeman Nickerson A request of Brother David Elliott to call on his Brother in Law Peter Warrin St. katherine upper Cannada Coburg Richard Lyman request of Uncle John [Smith]

5 October 1833—Saturday

this day started and Journy[ed] to the East came to Ashtibuly [Ashtabula, Ohio] stayed [at] Lambs tavern

6 October 1833—Sunday

arrived at Springfield [Erie County, Pennsylvania] on the Sabbath found the Brotheren in meeting Brother sidney [Rigdon] spoke to the people &c and in the Evening held a meeting at Brother Ruds [John Rudd] had a great congregation paid good attention Oh God Seal our te[s]timony to their hearts Amen /Continued at springfield untill tuesday the 8th [October 1833] Journeyed that day to br. Roundays [Shadrach Roundy] at Elk creek [Erie County, Pennsylvania] taried there over night came the next day to a tavern the next day thursday the 10th [October 1833] we ar[i]ved at Br Job Lewises at Westfield the breatheren by a previous appointment met there for meeting we spoke to them as the spirite gave utterence they were greatly gratifyed they appeared to be strong in the faith left there friday the 11 [October 1833] and came to the house of an infidel by the Name of Nash reasond with him but to no effect came Saturday the 12th [October 1833 to] the house of father Nicke[r]son I feel very well in my mind the Lord is with us but have much anxiety about my family &c;

13 October 1833—Sunday

held a meeting at freeman Nickerson['s] had a large congregation Brother Sidney preached & I bear record to the people the Lord gave his spirit in [a] marvilous maner for which I am thankful to the God of Ab[r]aham Lord bless my family and preserve them

14 October 1833—Monday

at the same place this day expect to start for Canada Lord be with us on our Journy Amen &c / Monday evening arived at Lodi [Cattaraugus County, New York] had an appointment preached to a small congregation made an appointment for tuesday at 10 oclock the 15th the meeting was appointed to be held in the Presbetarian meeting house but when the hour arived the man who kept the key of the house refused to open the door the meeting was thus prevented we came immedeately away and left the people in great confusion journeyed till friday [18 October 1833] Arived at Freeman Nickerson's in upper Canada having after we came into Canada passed through a very fine Country and well cultivated and had many peculiar feelings in relation to both the country and people we were kindly received at freeman Nickersons

20 October 1833—Sunday

held meeting at brantford on Sunday at 10 o clock to a very attentive congregation at candle lighting the same evening held meeting at mount plesent where freeman Nickerson lived to a very large congregation which gave good heed to the things which were spoken what may be the result we cannot tell but the p[r]ospect is flattering this morning Monday the [21 October 1833] enjoy pretty good health with good prospects of doing good calculate to stay in Canada till the Monday of next week then the Lord willing will start for home. left Mount plesent tuesday [22 October 1833] and arived at the village of Coulburn held meeting at candle lighting the evening was very bad snowing vehemently we were publickly opposed by a Wesleyen Methodist he was very tumultious but destitute of reason or knowledge he would not give us an oppertunity to reply this was on the 22nd [October 1833] we find that conviction is resting on the minds of some we hope that great good may yet be done in Canada which O Lord grant for thy names sake during our stay at mount plesent we [had] an interview with a Mr Wilkeson of the methodist order being a leader in that sect he could not stand against our words whether he will receive the truth the Lord only knows he seemed to [be] honest Written at Coulburn wednesday morning the 23 [October 1833] at the house of a Mr Bemer [Philip Beemer] left Mr Bemers on thursday 24 [October 1833] came to watterford held meeting at 1 o clock spoke to a small congregation being a very wet day after meeting returned to mount plesent and held meeting at candle lighting to a large congregation one man [Eleazer] Freeman Nickerson declared his full belief in the truth of the work is with his wife who is also convinced to be baptised on sunday great excitement prevailes in every place where we have been the result we leave in the hand of God. written at the house of Freeman Nickerson in mount plesent on friday morning the [25th October 1833] this afternoon at Mr Pattricks expect to hold a Meeting this Evening &c people very superstitious Oh God esta[b]lish thy word among this people held a meeting this evening had an attentive conngregation the spirit gave utterance

26 October 1833—Saturday

held a meeting at Mount Plasant the people very tender

/ 27 October 1833—Sunday

held a meeting in Mount plesent to a large congregation twelve came forward and was baptized and many more were deeply impressed appointed a meeting for this day

28 October 1833—Monday

at the request of some who desires to be baptized at candle lighting held a meeting for confirmation we broke bread laid on hands for the gift of the holy spirit had a good meeting the spirit was given in great power to some and the rest had great peace may God carry on his work in this place till all shall know him Amen. Held meeting yesterday at 10 o clock after meeting two came forward and were baptized confirmed them at the watters edge held meeting last evening ordained br E[leazer] F[reeman] Nickerson to the office of Elder had a good meeting one of the sisters got the gift of toungues which made the saints rejoice may God increse the gifts among them for his sons sake this morning we bend our course for home may the Lord prosper our journey Amen

29 October 1833—Tuesday

left Mountpleasant for home

30 October 1833—Wednesday

continued on our Journy Wensday and on

31 October 1833—Thursday

thirsday arrived at Buffalo

/ 1 November 1833—Friday Nove

Left Buffalo, N. Y. at 8 o'clock A.M. and arrived at home Monday, the 4th [November 1833] at 10, A.M. found my family all well according to the promise of the Lord, for which blessing I feel to thank his holy name; Amen.

13 November 1833—Wednesday

nothing of note transpired from the 4th of Nove[m]ber u[n]til this day in the morning at 4 Oh clock I was awoke by Brother Davis knocking at my door saying Brother

Joseph come git up and see the signs in the heavens and I arrose and beheld to my great Joy the stars fall from heaven yea they fell like hail stones a litteral fullfillment of the word of God as recorded in the holy scriptures and a sure sign that the coming of Christ is clost at hand Oh how marvellous are thy works Oh Lord and I thank thee for thy me[r]cy unto me thy servent Oh Lord save me in thy kingdom for Christ sake Amen

19 November 1833—Tuesday

from the 13th u[n]till this date nothing of note has transpired since the great sign in the heavins this day my h[ea]rt is somewhat sorrowfull but feel to trust in the Lord the god of Jacob I have learned in my travels that man is treche[r]ous and selfish but few excepted Brother Sidney is a man whom I love but is not capa[b]le of that pure and stedfast love for those who are his benefactors as should posess the breast of a President of the Chu[r]ch of Christ this with some other little things such as a selfish and indipendance of mind which to often manifest distroys the confidence of those who would lay down their lives for him but notwithstanding these things he is a very great and good man a man of great power of words and can gain the friendship of his hearrers very quick he is a man whom god will uphold if he will continue faithful to his calling O God grant that he may for the Lords sake Amen the man who willeth to do well we should extoll his virtues and speak not of his faults behind his back a man who willfuly turneth away from his friend without a cause is not easily forgiven the kindness of a man should is never to be forgotten that person who never forsaketh his trust should ever have the highest place for regard in our hearts and our love should never fail but increase more and more and this [is] my disposition and sentiment &c Amen Brother Frederick [G. Williams] is one of those men in whom I place the greatest confidence and trust for I have found him ever full of love and

Brotherly kindness he is not a man of many words but is ever wining because of his constant mind he shall ever have place in my heart and is ever intitled to my confidence / He is perfectly honest and upright, and seeks with all his heart to magnify his presidency in the church of ch[r]ist, but fails in many instances, in consequence of a want of confidence in himself: God grant that he mayovercome all evil: Blessed be brother Frederick, for he shall never want a friend; and his generation after him shall flourish. The Lord hath appointed him an inheritance upon the land of Zion. Yea, and his head shall blossom And he shall be as an olive branch that is bowed down with fruit: even so; Amen. And again, blessed be brother Sidney, also notwithstanding he shall be high and lifted up, yet he shall bow down under the yoke like unto an ass that coucheth beneath his burthen; that learneth his master's will by the stroke of the rod: thus saith the Lord. Yet the Lord will have mercy on him, and he shall bring forth much fruit; even as the vine of the choice grape when her clusters are is ripe, before the time of the gleaning of the vintage: and the Lord shall make his heart merry as with sweet wine because of him who putteth forth his hand and lifteth him up out of [a] deep mire, and pointeth him out the way, and guideth his feet when he stumbles; and humbleth him in his pride. Blessed are his generations. Nevertheless, one shall hunt after them as a man hunteth after an ass that hath strayed in the wilderness, & straitway findeth him and bringeth him into the fold. Thus shall the Lord watch over his generation that they may be saved: even so; Amen. / on the 13th and 14th days of October [1833] I baptised the following person[s] in Mount Pleasant viz

Moses Chapman Nickerson
Eleser [Eleazer] Freeman Nickerson
Prechard [Richard] Ramon Stowbridge [Strobridge]
Andrew Rose
Harvey John Cooper

Samuel Mc Alester [McAllister]
Eliza [McAllister] Nickerson
Mary Gates
Mary Birch [Burtch]
Lidia Baeley [Lydia Goldthwait Bailey Knight]
Elisabeth Gibbs
Phebe [Andrews] Cook
Margrett Birch [Burtch]
Esthe[r] Birch [Burtch]

25 November 1833—Monday

Brother Orson Hyde & John Gould returned from Zion and brough[t] the melencholly intelegen[ce] of the riot in Zion with the inhabitants in pers[ec]uting the brethren.

4 December 1833—Wednesday

commenced distributing the type and commenced setting on the 6 [December 1833] and being prepared to commence our Labours in the printing buisness I ask God in the name of Jesus to establish it for ever and cause that his word may speedily go for[th to] the Nations of the earth to the accomplishing of his great work in bringing about the restoration of the house of Israel

22 November 1833—Friday

my brother [Don] Carlos Smith came to live with me and also learn the printing art on the 9 of Dec[ember 1833] bro Phi[neas] Young came to board with me to board rent & lodge at one dollar & twenty five cents p[er] week Bro [Solomon] Wilbor Denton came to board 11 Dec[ember 1833] at one Dollar and twenty five cents per week.

18 December 1833—Wednesday

This day the Elders assembled togeth[er] in the printing office and then proceded to bow down before the Lord and dedicate the printing press and all that pertains thereunto to God by mine own hand and confirmed by bro Sidney Rigdon and Hyrum Smith and then proceded to take the first proof sheet of the star edited by Bro Oliv[er] Cowd[er]y blessed of the Lord is bro Oliver nevertheless there are two evils in him that he must needs forsake or he cannot altogeth[er] escape the buffitings of the adver[sar]y if he shall forsak[e] these evils he shall be forgiven and shall be made like unto the bow which the Lord hath set in the heavens he shall be a sign and an ensign unto the nations. behold he is blessed of the Lord for his constancy and steadfastness in the work of the Lord wherefore he shall be blessed in his generation and they shall never be cut off and he shall be helped out of many troubles and if he keep the commandments and harken unto the council of the Lord [and] his rest shall be glorious and again blessed of the Lord is my father and also my mother and my brothers and my sisters for they shall yet find redemption in the house of the Lord and their ofsprings shall be a blessing a Joy and a comfort unto them blessed is my mother for her soul is ever fill[ed] with benevolence and phylanthropy and notwithstanding her age yet she shall receive strength and shall be comferted in the midst of her house and she shall have eternal life and blessed is my father for the hand of the Lord shall be over him for he shall see the affliction of his children pass away and when his head is fully ripe he shall behold himself as an olive tree whose branches are bowed down with much fruit he shall also possess a mansion on high blessed of the Lord is my brother Hyrum for the integrity of his heart he shall be girt about with truth and faithfulness shall be the strength of his loins from generation to generation he shall be a shaft in the hand of his God to exicute Judgment upon his enemies and he shall be hid by the hand of the Lord that none of his secret parts shall be discovered unto his hu[r]t his name shall be accounted a blessing among men and when he is in trouble and great tribulation hath come upon him he shall remember the God of Jacob and he will shield him from the power of satan and he shall receive councel in the house of the most high that he may be streng[t]hened in hope that the going of his feet may be established for eve[r] blessed of the Lord is bro Samuel [Harrison Smith] because the Lord shall say unto him Sam[ue]l, Sam[ue]l, therefore he shall be made a teache[r] in the house of the Lord and the Lord shall mature his mind in Judgment and thereby he shall obtain the esteem and fellowship of his brethren and his soul shall be established and he shall benefit the house of the Lord because he shall obtain answer to prayer in his faithfulness Bro William [Smith] is as the fi[e]rce Lion who devideth not the spoil because of his strength and in the pride of his heart he will neglect the more weighty matters until his soul is bowed down in sorrow and then he shall return and call on the name of his God and shall find forgiveness and shall wax valient therefor he shall be saved unto the utter most and as the roaring Lion of the forest in the midst of his prey so shall the hand of his generation be lifted up against those who are set on high that fight against the God of Israel fearless and unda[u]nted shall they be in battle in avenging the rongs of the innocent and relieving the oppressed therfor the blessings of the God of Jacob shall be in the midst of his house notwithstanding his rebelious heart and now O God let the residue of my fathers house ever come up in remembrance before thee that thou mayest save them from the hand of the oppressor and establish their feet upon the rock of ages that they may have place in thy house and be saved in thy Kingdom and let all these things be even as I have said for Christs sake Amen

19 December 1833—Thursday

This day Bro William Pratt and David Pattin [Patten] took their Journey to the Land of Zion for the purpose of bearing dispatches to the Brethren in that place from Kirtland O may God grant it a blessing for Zion as a kind Angel from heaven Amen

1834

January 16th 1834

this night at Brother Jinkins [Wilkins Jenkins] Salisbury['s] came from home Oh Lord keep us and my Family safe untill I can return to them again Oh my God have mercy on my Bretheren in Zion for Christ Sake Amen

/ January 11, 1834.

This evening Joseph Smith Jr, Frederick G. Williams, Newel K. Whitney, John Johnson, Oliver Cowdery, and Orson Hyd[e] united in prayer and asked the Lord to grant the following petition: Firstly, That the Lord would grant that our lives might be precious in his sight, that he would watch over our persons and give his angels charge concerning us and our families that no evil nor unseen hand might be permitted to harm us. Secondly, That the Lord would also hold the lives of all the United firm, and not suffer that any of them shall be taken. Thirdly, That the Lord would grant that our brother Joseph might prevail over his enemy, even Docter P. Hurlbut, who has threatened his life, whom brother Joseph has caused to be taken with a precept; that the Lord would fill the heart of the court with a spirit to do justice, and cause that the law of the land may be magnified in bringing him to justice. Fourthly, That the Lord would provide, in the order of his Providence, the bishop of this church with means sufficient to discharge every debt that the Firm owes, in due season, that the Church may not be braught into disrepute, and the saints be afflicted by the hands of their enemies. Fifthly, That the Lord would protect our printing press from the hands of evil men, and give us means to send forth his word, even his gospel that the ey ears of all may hear it, and also that we may print his scriptures, and also that he would give those who were appointed to conduct the press, wisdom sufficient that the cause may not be hindered, but that men's eyes may thereby be opened to see the truth. Sixthly, That the Lord would deliver Zion, and gather in his scattered people, to possess it in peace; and also, while in their dispersion, that he would provide for them that they perish not with hunger nor cold. And finally, that God in the name of Jesus would gather his elect speedily, and unveil his face that his saints might behold his glory and dwell with him; Amen. On the 13th of March A. D. 1833, Docter P. Hurlbut came to my house; I conversed with him considerably about the book of Mormon. He was ordained to the office of an elder in this Church under the hand of Sidney Rigdon on the 18th of March in the same year above written. According to my best recollection, I heard him say, in the course of conversing with him, that if he ever became convinced that the book of Mormon was false, he would be the cause of my destruction, &c. He was tried before a counsel of high priests on the 21st day of June, 1833, and his license restored to him again, it he previously having been cut off from the Church by the bishop's court. He was finally cut off from the church a few days after having his license restored, on the 21st of June. / and then saught the distruction of the saints in this place and more particularly myself and family and as the Lord has in his mercy Delivered me out of his hand till the present and also the church that he has not prevailed viz the 28 day of Jany 1834 for which I off[er] the gratitud[e] of my heart to Allmighty God for the same and on this night Bro Oliv[er] and bro Frederick and my self bowed before the Lord being agred and united in pray[er] that God would continue to deliver me and my brethren from him that he may not prevail again[st] us in the law suit that is pending and also that God would soften down the hearts of E[lijah] Smith J[osiah] Jones Lowd [Austin Loud] & [Azariah] Lyman and also [Andrew] Bardsly that they might obey the gospel or if they would not repent that the Lord would send faithful saints to purchase their farms that this stake may be strengthened and its borders enlarged

/ 31 January 1834—Friday

it is my prayer to the Lord that three thousand subscriber[s] may be added to the Star in the term of three yea[rs]

26 February 1834—Wednesday

started from home to obtain volenteers for Zion

27 February 1834—Thursday

startted Started stayed at Br Roundays

28 February 1834—Friday

stayed at a strangers who entertained us very kindly in Westleville [Wesleyville, Erie County, Pennsylvania]

1 March 1834—Saturday

arived at Br [Job] Lewis and on the 2d [March 1834] the Sabath Brother Barly [Parley Pratt] preached in this place and I preached in the evening had a good meeting there is a small church in this place tha[t] seem to be strong in th[e] faith Oh may God keep them in the faith and save them and lead them to Zion

3 March 1834—Monday

this morning intend[ed] to start on our Journy to the east But did not start O may God bless us with the gift of utterance to accomplish the Journy and the Errand on which we are sent and return soon to the land of Kirtland and find my Family all well O Lord bless my little children with health and long life to do good in th[is] generation for Christs sake Amen /Kirtland Geauger [Geauga County] Ohio

Thom[p]son [Geauga County]
Springfield Erie [County] Pensy[l]
Elkcrick [Elk Creek, Erie County] vania
Westfield [Chautauqua, New York]
Laona Chautauque N york
Silver Creek [Chautauqua, New York]
Perysburgh Cateragus [Cattaraugus County, New York]
Collins Genesee [County, New York]
China [Genesee County, New York]
Warsaw [Genesee County, New York]
Geneseeo
Levingston [Geneseo, Livingston County, New York]
Sentervill [Centreville, Allegany County, New York]
Cattlin Alleghany
Spafford
Onondaga [County, New York]
John Gould payed me on papers $ 1.50 /Journal of P[arley Pratt] and J[oseph Smith]

4, 5 March 1834—Tuesday, Wednesday

took our Journy from Westfield [Chatauqua County, New York] accompanied By Br [John] gould rode 33 miles arrived in staid all night with a Brother [Reuben] Mc Bride, next morning went 4 m[ile]s to Br Nicisons [Freeman Nickerson's] found him and his house hold full of faith and of the holy spirit we cald the church together and Related unto them what had hapened to our Brethren in Zion opened to them the prophesyes and revelations concerning the order of the gethering of Zion and the means of her Redemtion and Brother Joseph Prophesyed to them and the spirit of the Lord came mightily upon them and with all redyness the yo[u]ng and middle aged volenteered for Zion same evening held 2 meetings 3 or 4 miles Apart.

6 March 1834—Thursday

next day March 6th [1834] held another Meeting at Bro Nicisons the few un Believeers that atended were outragious and the meeting ended in compleet confusion

7 March 1834—Friday

started on our Journy accompanyed By Br Nicison Leaving Brs goold [John Gould] and Mathews to Prepare and gether up the companys in the churches in that region and meet us in Ohio Reddy for Zion the first of May we arrived after dark to the county seat of Cataraugus cald Elicutville [Ellicottville] tryed every tavern in the place But Being Court time we found no room But were compeled to ride on in a d dark muddy rainy night we found shelter in rideing 1 mile Paid higher for our fare than tavern price

8 March 1834—Saturday

continued our journy came to Palmersville [Farmersville] to the house of Elder Mc gown [Marcellus McKown] were Invited to go to Esq to spend the evening we found them verry friendly and somewhat Believeing tarryed allnight

9 March 1834—Sunday

held meeting in a school house had great attentian found a few desyples who were firm in faith and after meeting found many Believeing and could hardly get away from them we apointed A meeting in freedom [Cattaraugus County, New York] for Monday 10th [March 1834] and are now at Mr [Warren A.] Cowderyes in the full Enjoyment of all the Blessings Both temporal and spiritual of which we stand in need or are found worthy to receive held meting on Monday Preachd to crowd[ed] congregat[ion] at eve preacht again to a hous crowded full to overflowing after meting I proposed if any wished to obey if they would make it manifest we would stay to administer at another meeting a young man of the methodist order arose and testified his faith in the fulness of the gospel and desired to Be Baptised we Appointed another meting and the nextday tuesday 11th [March 1834] held meeting and Baptised Heman hide after which we rode 9 m[ile]s Put up with ....next day rode 36 m[ile]s to fauther [Edmund] Bosleys.

13 March 1834—Thursday

held meting I Preachd

14 March 1834—Friday

in F[ather Alvah] Beamans

15 March 1834—Saturday

at Father Beamans and Brother Sidny [Rigdon] and Lyman [Wight] arived at his house to the Joy of our Souls in Lyvona [Livonia, Livingston County, New York]

16 March 1834—Sunday

Brother Sidney preached to a very large congregation in Geneseo

17 March 1834—Monday

Brother Parly preached in the afternoon

18 March 1834—Tuesday

Stayed at Father Boslys [Edmund Bosley] all day

19 March 1834—Wednesday

Started for home arrived at Brother Whitheys [Isaac McWithy] tarried all night &c

20 March 1834—Thursday

Started on our Journy at noon took dinner at Brother Joseph Holbrooks, and at night tryed three times to git keept in the name of Deciples, and could not be keept, after night we found a man who would keep us for mony thus we see that there is more pl place for mony than for Jesus Deciples or the Lamb of God, the name of the man is Wilson Rauben Wilson Reuben Wilson that would not keep us without mony he lived in China [Genesee County, New York] &c.

21 March 1834—Friday

came to a man by the name of Starks 6th miles East of Springville [Erie County, New York]

22 March 1834—Saturday

came and tarri[e]d with vincen nights [Vinson Knight] in Perrysburg Co of Cattaraugus

23 March 1834—Sunday

came to Father [Freeman] Nickersons Perrysburg the same Co[unty] NY held a meeting &c.

24 March 1834—Monday

This day am not able to start for home but feel determined to go on the morrow morning

25 March 1834—Tuesday

came from Father Nickerson to Father Leweses [Job Lewis] in Westfield [Chautauqua Co., New York] Father Nickerson came with me

26 March 1834—Wednesday

Came from Westfield to Elk kreek [Erie County, Pennsylvania] stayed with Elder Hunt on free cost

27 March 1834—Thursday

came to springfield [Pennsylvania] found Brother Sidney and came to within 16 miles from Painsville

28 March 1834—Friday

Came home found my Family all well and the Lord be praised for this blessing

29 March 1834—Saturday

at home had much Joy with my Family

30 March 1834—Sunday

Sabbath at home and went to hear Brother Sidney Preach the word of life &c.

31 March 1834—Monday

Monday this day came to Sharden [Chardon, Geauga County, Ohio] to tend the Court against Docter P Hurlbut &c

1 April 1834—Tuesday

this day at Brother Riders and the Court has not braught on our tryal yet we are ingaged in makeing out some supenies [subpoenas] &c for witnesses this is Ap[r]el 1st Tusday my soul delighteth in the Law of the Lord for he forgiveth my sins and will confound mine Enimies the Lord shall destroy him who has lifted his heel against me even that wicked man Docter P. H[u]rlbut he will deliver him to the fowls of heaven and his bones shall be cast to the blast of the wind for he lifted his arm against the Almity therefore the Lord shall destroy him

/ 2 April 1834—Wednesday

attended court at Chardon,

3 April 1834—Thursday

the same.

4 April 1834—Friday

morning returned home.

5 April 1834—Saturday

returned to Chardon as witness for fath[er John] Johnson in the evening returned home. Mr. Bussle [Benjamin Bissel] the State's Att'y for Portage County called on me this evening: He is a gentlemanly appearing man, and treated me with respect.

/ April 1834—Monday

Bros Newel Oliver Frederick Heber [Kimball] and myself meet in the counsel room and bowed down befor[e] the Lord and prayed that he would furnish the means to deliver the firm from debt and be set at liberty and also that I may prevail against that wicked Hurlbut and that he be put to shame accordingly on the 9 [April 1834] after an impartial trial the Court decided that the said Hurlbut was bound over under 200 dollars bond to keep the peace for six month[s] and pay the cost which amounted to near three hundred dollars all of which was in answer to our prayer for which I thank my heavenly father Remember to carry the bond between A S Gilbert & N K Whitney and have them exchanged when I go to Zion

10 April 1834—Thursday

had a co[u]ncel of the united firm at which it was agreed that the firm should be desolv[ed] and each one have their stewardship set off to them

11 April 1834—Friday

attended meeting and restored Father Tyler to the Church

12 April 1834—Saturday

went to the lake [Erie] and spent the day in fishing and visiting the brethren in that place and took my horse from Father [John] Johnson and let brother Frederick [G. Williams] have him to keep.

13 April 1834—Sunday

was sick and could not attend meeting

14 April 1834—Monday

purch[as]ed some hay and oats and got them home

15 April 1834—Tuesday

drawed a load of hay & on Wednesday 16 [April 1834] plowed and sowed oats for Brother Frederick and on

17 April 1834—Thursday

attended a meeting agreeable to appoint[ment] at which time the important subjects of the deliverence of Zion and the building of the Lords house in Kirtland by bro Sidney after which bro Joseph arose and requested the brethren and sisters to contr[i]bute all the money they could for the deliverence of Zion and received twenty nine dollars and sixty eight cts

/ 18 April 1834—Friday

left Kirtland in company with brothers Sidney Rigdon, Oliver Cowdery, and Zebedee Coltrin for New Portage to attend a conference. Travelled to W[illiam]. W. Williams in Newburgh [Cuyahoga County, Ohio] and took dinner, after which we travelled on, and after dark were hailed by a man who desired to ride. We were checked by the Spirit and refused: he professed to be sick; but in a few minutes was joined by two others who followed us hard, cursing and swearing, but we were successful in escaping their hands through the providence of the Lord, and stayed at a tavern where we were treated with civility. Next morning,

19 April 1834—Saturday

started, and arrived at brother Joseph Bozworth's [Bosworth] in Copley, Medina County, [Ohio] where we took dinner. Bro. J. Bozworth was strong in the faith he is a good man and may, if faithful, do much good. After resting a while, we left, and soon arrived at brother Johnathan Tayler's [Jonathan Taylor], in Norton, where we were received with kindness. We soon retired to the wilderness where we united in prayer and suplication for the blessings of the Lord to be given unto his church: We called upon the Father in the name of Jesus to go with the breth[r]en who were going up to the land of Zion, to give brother Joseph strength, and wisdom, and understanding sufficient to lead the people of the Lord, and to gather back and establish the saints upon the land of their inheritances, and organize them according to the will of heaven, that they be no more cast down forever. We then united and laid on hands: Brothers Sidney, Oliver, and Zebedee [Coltrin] laid hands upon bro. Joseph, and confirmed upon him all the blessings necessary to qualify him to stand before the Lord in his high calling; and he return again in peace and triumph, to enjoy the society of his breth[r]en. Brothers Joseph, Sidney, and Zebedee then laid hands upon bro. Oliver, and confirmed upon him the blessings of wisdom and understanding sufficient for his station; that he be qualified to assist brother Sidney in arranging the church covenants which are to be soon published; and to have intelligence in all things to do the work of printing. Brother[s] Joseph, Oliver, Zebedee then laid hands upon bro. Sidney, and confirmed upon him the blessings of wisdom and knowledge to preside over the Church in the abscence of brother Joseph, and to have the spirit to assist bro. Oliver in conducting the Star, and to arrange the Church covenants, and the blessing of old age and peace, till Zion is built up & Kirtland established, till all his enemies are under his feet, and of a crown of eternal life in the Kingdom of God with us. We, Joseph, Sidney, and Oliver then laid hands upon bro. Zebedee, and confirmed the blessing of wisdom to preach the gospel, even till it spreads to the islands of the sea, and to be spared to see three score years and ten, and see Zion built up and Kirtland established forever, and even at last to receive a crown of life. Our hearts rejoiced, and we were comforted with the Holy Spirit, Amen.

20 April 1834—Sunday

Brother Sidney Rigdon entertained a large congregation of saints, with an interesting discourse upon the "Dispensation of the fulness of times," &c.

21 April 1834—Monday

Attended conference and had a glorious time, some few volunteered to go to Zion, and others donated $66.37 for the benefit of the scattered breth[r]en in Zion.

22 April 1834—Tuesday

Returned to Kirtland on the 22d and found all well.

23 April 1834—Wednesday

Assembled in council with breth[r]en Sidney, Frederick, Newel, John Johnson and Oliver and united in asking the Lord to give bro. Zebedee Coltrin influence over our bro. Jacob Myre [Myers], and obtain from him the money which he has gone to borrow for us, or cause him to come to this place & give it himself.

/ 30 April 1834—Wednesday

this day paid the amount sum of fifty dollars on the following memorandom to the following persons viz

Milton Holmes	$15.00
Henry Herriman	7.00
Sylvester Smith	10.00
Wm Smith	5.00

Harvey Stanl[e]y	5.00
William Smith	5.00
N K Whitney	3.00
	$50.00

Money received of the following brethren consecrated for the deliver[y] of Zion

By letter from East	$10.00
Do" [ditto]	50.00
Do"	100.00
By Letter	$07.00
Wm Smith	5.00
Wm Cahoon	5.00
Harvey Stanley	5.00
Received of Martin Harris	47.00
/Rec[e]ived of Dexter Stillman	10.
Doof Lyman Johnson	5.00
Doof Sophia Howe	7.60

/ 21 August 1834—Thursday

This day brother Frederick Williams returned from Cleveland and told us concerning the plague, and after much consultation we agreed that bro. Frederick should go to Cleveland and commence administering to the sick, for the purpose of obtaining blessings for them, and blessings for them, and for the glory of the Lord: Accordingly we, Joseph, Frederick, and Oliver united in prayer before the Lord for this thing. Now, O Lord, grant unto us this blessing, in the name of Jesus Christ, and thy name shall have the glory forever; Amen.

30 August 1834—Saturday

Received of the Church by the hand of Jared Carter from the east of consecrated money $3.00

4 September 1834—Thursday

This day Edward [Edmund] Bosley said that if he could obtain the management of his property in one year he would put it in for the printing of the word of the Lord.

29 November 1834—Friday

This evening Joseph and Oliver united in prayer for the continuance of blessings, after giving thanks for the relief which the Lord had lately sent us by opening the hearts of certain brethren from the east to loan us $430. After conversing and rejoicing before the Lord on this occasion we agreed to enter into the following covenant with the Lord, viz: That if the Lord will prosper us in our business, and open the way before us that we may obtain means to pay our debts, that we be not troubled nor brought into disrepute before the world nor his people, that after that of all that he shall give us we will give a tenth, to be bestowed upon the poor in his Church, or as he shall command, and that we will be faithful over that which he has entrusted to our care that we may obtain much: and that our children after us shall remember to observe this sacred and holy covenant: And that our children and our children's [children] may know of the same we here subscribe our names with our own hands before the Lord: /Oliver Cowdery. And now, O Father, as thou didst prosper our father Jacob, and bless him with protection and prosperity where ever he went from the time he made a like covenant before and with thee; and as thou didst, even the same night, open the heavens unto him and manifest great mercy and favor, and give him promises, so wilt thou do by us his sons; and as his blessings prevailed above the blessings of his Progenitors unto the utmost bounds of the everlasting hills, even so may our blessings prevail like his; and may thy servants be preserved from the power and influence of wicked and unrighteous men; may every weapon formed against us fall upon the head of him who shall form it; may we be blessed with a name and a place among thy saints here, and thy sanctified when they shall rest. Amen.

30 November 1834—Sunday

While reflecting upon the goodness and mercy of the Lord, this evening, a prophecy was put into our hearts, that in a short time the Lord would arrange his providences in a merciful manner and send us assistance to deliver us from debt and bondage.

5 December 1834—Friday

According to the directions of the Holy Spirit breth[r]en Joseph Smith Jr. Sidney, Frederick G. Williams, and Oliver Cowdery, assembled to converse upon the welfare of the Church, when brother Oliver Cowdery was ordained an assistant President of the High and Holy Priesthood under the hands of brother Joseph Smith Jr. saying, "My brother, in the name of Jesus Christ who was crucified for the sins of the world, I lay my hands upon thee, and ordain thee an assistant President of the high and holy priesthood in the Church of the Latter Day Saints["] /Please to send the Paper that Has formerly Been sent to John C|. .|p|. .|ton send it Now to Nathan Chase at West Lodi Cataraugus County N. Y Received of Elisha C Hubbard one Dollar for Papers Perysburgh Hazard Andr[e]ws 1 paper Fairview Postoffi[ce] Cattaragus County I have sent the money 25 cents by David M|.|t|. .| as he was to send the paper to Mis Taylor to Rushford but I wish to have it come in my name as above Direct Samuel Mcbride & James Mcbride['s] Papers to Nashville Post office Shitauqua County I wish you to send me one more Paper monthly and send one

Monthly Paper to Eleazer & Samuel & Richard Nickerson South Dennis in the County of Barnstable Massachusetts J[ohn] Nickerson /The voice of the Spirit is, that brother Sidney speak to the congregation this day, first, Brother Joseph next, bro. Oliver and if time bro Zebedee [Coltrin] Joseph Smith Jr

Oliver Cowdery

www.ingramcontent.com/pod-product-compliance
Lightning Source LLC
LaVergne TN
LVHW041503070426
835507LV00009B/791